Push
The Tarp

A story about fostering authentic
leadership and great teams.

TIM McMAHON

1

PRAISE FOR *PUSH THE TARP*

"Wow. What a story! This book brought me to tears three different times. I could feel myself in the story. We've all been looking for a mentor like Rusty. We also all need *to be* a mentor like Rusty. This is a must read."

Brian Cain, MPM
Mental Performance Coach

"Leading teams effectively is a critical skill, needed now more than ever. Through his storytelling, Tim McMahon outlines a concise roadmap to develop methods and engage your team. Dig in to *Push the Tarp*."

Ann McKenzie, MSN, RN,
Director of College Relations, Villanova University M.
Louise Fitzpatrick College of Nursing

"Push the Tarp is genuine leadership that translates to any industry or team. What Tim brings out most in this story, however, is the power of relationships and the lasting impact we can all have on each other on our respective journeys...when we push the tarp."

Jay Artinian
Deputy Director of Athletics, Hofstra University

When we were 15 and 16 years old, my mom would drive me, Tim, and our fellow teammate, Joe, to summer baseball games all over Long Island.

I'm talking four weekday games, and double-headers on Saturdays on Sundays. My mom always loved Tim. She laughed at all his goofy jokes; he always had something sweet to say to her, and she often talked about him.

As I read this book, and as completely relatable as it is to many kids who are ages 12 to 22, I also better understand the connection he had with my mom. As his teammate, I saw him stay positive—but I also saw him struggle.

He was never the most talented player but always competed to be his best. What I recall from those years is the work ethic and the manner in which he carried himself.

If you have a son or daughter who is struggling or who is thriving, this book can help.

This book comes from a perspective of someone who was wise before his years, who was a great teammate and who has become a trusted leader in his field. The manner in which he captures and harnesses his own adolescent and teen anxieties into the inspiring story of Jimmy and Rusty is spot on.

Push the Tarp is a story that brings to the forefront emotions and dynamics that kids and parents, teammates and colleagues, are often dealing with and working through. And, it provides a framework to be the best leader and teammate you can be on your own journey.

My mom passed away last year, and while I wish she had the chance to read *Push the Tarp*, I have no doubt she helped write a few pages from all of those car rides many years ago.

Rich Ciancimino
Co-Host and Executive Producer
"The Mayor's Office with Sean Casey"
11-Time Emmy-Award–Winning Sports TV Producer

It happened so quickly I couldn't get out of the way. I've turned away from so many pitches like that one. The ball would normally hit me in my back and I would be running to first base thinking of how I was going to steal second and third. I didn't react like I had in the past and this pitch hit my wrist—hard. Before I knew it, I was shaking my wrist and was greeted by a sharp, throbbing pain I had never felt before.

As I waited in the athletic trainer's room to get the results of the X-ray, I couldn't help but think of everything I was about to miss out on if my wrist was broken: an invitation to a top summer wood-bat league, a chance to play in front of professional scouts, and a fun summer with teammates from other college baseball programs in a part of the country where I had never been but always dreamed of going.

"Well, Jimmy, I'm sorry, but it's a clear break," said my trainer, Mike. "Frankly, you're lucky it isn't worse. We'll need to get you in a cast, and I'm afraid your season and your summer league goals are over."

Mike would be the captain of the truth-teller's club if there were one. I appreciated the way he took care of me and my teammates, but I was hoping he would have better news for me that day.

Before I could even call my parents, Coach Delancey walked in. He received Mike's text that it was a clean break. "I'm sorry, Jimmy. There's no way around this bad news. It stinks. Look at it this way: you still have your senior year to prove yourself to the professional scouts," Coach Delancey said. "You think you'll go home for the summer now that the summer collegiate wood-bat league is out of the question?"

I loved my hometown and all of my childhood friends, but I was really looking forward to this summer league experience. "I guess so, Coach," I said. "I was hoping not to clear tables at Regent's Row this summer. It's a great restaurant with amazing people, except...."

"Well, call your folks, get this wrist in a cast and get some sleep," Coach Delancey said calmly. "Stop by my office tomorrow afternoon and we can talk through the best way to manage this situation. Remember, adversity can become your advantage if you let it."

As Coach walked out, I could hear Mike on the phone with the hospital. I knew I had to call my parents and share the news that I would be living at home this summer, after all. I could hear my mom at first very concerned about my wrist, and then trying to mask her excitement that I would be staying home.

I knew my dad would immediately find the silver lining in this. I wasn't ready for that talk yet. I was caught in my own thoughts, feeling sorry for myself and thinking of everything I was about to miss out on in Wisconsin.

My junior baseball season was over, my summer league never started, and there was no guarantee my wrist would ever be the same.

When I arrived at the hospital, my parents met me in the ER. They lived about 15 miles from campus. The game I was injured in was one of only three home games they missed all year. With them by my side (as they always were), the physician's assistant took a closer look and deemed this break worse than Mike had initially thought.

Instead of three to five weeks, this cast would be on for six to eight weeks and then I would start rehabilitation to bring back my range of motion, flexibility and strength before I'd be able to step into the batter's box again. My parents drove me back to campus and dropped me off at Coach Delancey's office.

"Six to eight weeks," I said as I slumped into a chair across the desk from him.

Now I was really feeling sorry for myself. I came to play at Hofstra University because of Coach D (which is what everyone called Coach Delancey). One of the things I liked most about him was that he cared for his players on and off the field. Little did I know, while I was wallowing in "why me?" he was about to change my life.

He ignored my news and body language entirely. "Jimmy! Great news!" Coach said. "I spoke with Coach Harrison at the Mequon Chinooks, the team in the Wisconsin Summer Collegiate League (WSCL) that you were going to play for this summer. He agreed to hire you as a member of their grounds crew. We have been friends for years since our own WSCL summer ball days and I told him you're a good kid who had a bad break—. Sorry, I couldn't help myself, pal."

Coach was making jokes and I was not sure he heard me share my news. I started to say it again before he interrupted me with "I heard you, pal. Six to eight weeks. GOOD! That gives you one full month on their grounds crew to learn new things from different people and from a different perspective. You'll also meet new friends, form new relationships, and earn a couple bucks. The host family that was planning to have you at their home for the summer also said they would continue to do so!"

Coach D was big on relationships...and always looking at things from all angles. I didn't get it. My attitude was still in the dumps and I was thinking, *Why would the Chinooks want to hire me with a bum wrist, anyway?*

"Jimmy, listen here. I was going to save this conversation for our end-of-season wrap-up, but let's do it now. The truth is, you haven't been yourself this season. Your head seems to be thinking of a million thoughts all at once and therefore, you are stuck in thought and not in the moment. It's like you live with one foot in the past and one in the future, and never stand fully in the present.

"You seem to have no plan in the batter's box and your struggles at bat have followed you into the field and into the locker room with your teammates. You were our most sure-handed infielder until this season, too. "In fact, I believe if you were more present—in the moment—you would never have gotten hit on the wrist by that pitch yesterday. While I'm at it, Adrienne in academic advising called me on Friday and shared that you missed your last advising session, and your grades have been slipping. We talked about how you do anything is how you do everything, and this is just another example of that, only in the opposite direction of where we want to go."

Coach paused, knowing he was giving a lot to me straight. "I want you to seriously consider taking this job at the Chinooks and find the best version of yourself—the energetic, hungry team leader on and off the field who we know.

"I care about you, Jimmy, and that's why I called Coach Harrison to ask for some creative options for your development this summer. Now it's on you to make the most of it. Stop feeling sorry for yourself: it's a useless emotion that does nothing productive for you, so let's turn the page."

I was frustrated by Coach D's feedback at that moment. Baseball always came easy to me; I never had to work very hard at anything. As I look back, I never had much adversity on the field or in the classroom until I broke my wrist. School was easy but as I started to take harder courses during my junior year, it required greater focus and more hours of work. Oddly, as I stood up, I thanked him for his honest feedback and support and walked toward the hallway, processing the healthy dose of candor from Coach D.

Before I left, I turned around and asked him one question.

"Coach, why did you say "Good!" after I told you it would be six to eight weeks? What's *good* about that?"

His answer has stayed with me to this day, in that he didn't give me one. He only said, "Time to pack your bags for Wisconsin and find out."

CHAPTER 3
WISCONSIN

I had one week until the WSCL season began. We ended the collegiate season in fifth place and with the top four teams advancing to the conference playoffs; our season ended one week after my injury.

Once finals wrapped up, I went home to see my family and my friends before joining the grounds crew for the Chinooks Baseball Club in Mequon, Wisconsin.

I didn't receive many details for the job except an email confirmation from Coach Harrison and a great phone call from the host family, the Bowmans, who seemed excited to have me.

I kept wondering how I would be a productive worker on the grounds crew with a broken wrist. As the day of my trip approached, I kept hearing Coach D saying "good!" and found myself getting increasingly curious.

After a smooth flight from LaGuardia to Milwaukee's General Mitchell airport, I met the Bowman family, including Meghan and Sally who were 12 and 11 years old, respectively. I settled into the Bowmans' guest bedroom and was in bed by 9 p.m. I was to arrive at the Chinooks ballpark by 7:30 the next morning.

Before I fell asleep, I felt grateful for Coach D and I was eager to see how this opportunity would unfold. Little did I know my job on the grounds crew was going to be nothing like I expected.

CHAPTER 4
RUSTY

If you're from the East Coast, you may never come to appreciate how beautiful Wisconsin is—especially in the summer. The Chinooks field is set off from Lake Michigan, high atop a bluff in the town of Mequon, about 20 minutes north of Milwaukee. I never realized how stunning the lake is, with turquoise water more akin to what one might expect in the Caribbean and not the upper Midwest.

I pulled into the lot next to the ballpark at 7:20 a.m. and recognized Coach Harrison from his picture on the Chinooks website. Coach Harry, as he was known, played summer ball years ago with Coach D, and their longtime friendship made this possible for me. I parked but didn't even have a chance to open my door before Harry was at the car, smiling wide to welcome me.

"You must be Jimmy! Can't miss you with that cast, my man. I'm sorry about your injury, and I won't do you the disservice of feeling sorry for you. I'm thrilled you said yes to this experience and I'm glad you're here.

"We were looking forward to coaching you up this summer and while I know you'd rather be playing and competing, this is going to be a great experience for you if you let it. C'mon, Rusty is eager to meet his grounds crew."

Before we walked to the field, I looked around and only saw my car, Harry's pickup and a bike resting up against the back of the third-base dugout. I started to wonder where the rest of the grounds crew was when Harry said, "We've never had a role like yours, Jimmy. We always simply cared for the field on our own. We feel it's important to teach ownership and that people don't get *down on* what they are *in on,* so we want everyone in on taking care of the field. However, since we have Rusty with us this summer, I jumped at the chance for you to work with him specifically—with him and maybe for him."

Before I could say anything, Harry energetically introduced me: "Rusty, here's your clay! I mean, Jimmy," he said laughing.

I was starting to get a feel for Harry's sense of humor, and it was oddly reminiscent of Coach D's.

"Jimmy, welcome," Rusty said kindly and firmly. "Let's get started...."

CHAPTER 5
GET TO THE TARP

Before I could ask why I was the only person on the grounds crew or why Harry referred to me as clay or what exactly was going on, Rusty showed me around. It was rather ordinary. He gave me keys to the field and as we walked around the crushed gravel that encircled the grass, he asked me about my family, my teammates and my favorite baseball players. I was lost in my own feelings, still wondering why I was his only "piece of clay." I didn't realize Rusty was, in his own way, welcoming me and trying to get to know me.

We walked the entire field, checked out the storage closets in each dugout and then Rusty came more alive when we stopped at the tarp along the left-field line.

For those not familiar with baseball or softball, each diamond (at least at the college level and above) has a synthetic covering in foul territory on the left or right field line that is rolled up on a large metal cylinder. Most attendees do not even notice it, resting up against a chain-link fence or brick wall. Even in my immature, confused state of mind, I could feel Rusty wanted to talk more about the tarp.

However, as he started to say something, he looked at his watch and realized it was 8:15 a.m. The Chinooks players started to arrive. "More on the tarp tomorrow, Jimmy. For now, please rake the pitcher's mound and home plate. The team starts practice at 8:30."

If you've played baseball (or any team sport for that matter), you know that the minutes before practice are some of the best moments of camaraderie and fun.

Even with my left wrist in a cast, it felt good to be in that moment. I raked the mound and home plate as best I could as the players arrived and bantered in the dugout.

I recognized a few of them from our school's college ball in the Northeast but most were from the Midwest, Texas and California.

As they hustled to the outfield to warm up and stretch, huge storm clouds blew in and Harry hollered at everyone to "Get to the tarp!"

CHAPTER 6
THE STORM

The summer storm clouds rolled in fast. Without much talking, everyone was at the tarp in less than a minute. I was pushing in the middle (with my good arm) and it was not until the infield was covered that I realized Rusty, Harry and the assistant coaches had also joined the crew. Even the marketing and promotions assistant, who had been putting seat cushions in the storage closet when the storm began, showed up to push.

As we secured the tarp over the infield with sandbags, Harry called the players into the third-base dugout for a team meeting. Rusty motioned at me and pointed to the stack of sandbags along the right field-line fence. That left me, aka the grounds crew, to finish securing the field with the rest of about 30 bags. I started in right field and worked my way around to the left field line.

As I came closer to the dugout where everyone was meeting, I realized Harry, his coaching staff and the team were listening to Rusty. I could hear some of what he was saying but didn't want to neglect my job at the moment with the sandbags.

I continued working my way around the covering, dropping bags where needed, and did my best to hear what Rusty was saying, but the batting practice music was playing and it was hard to hear Rusty through *Start Me Up* and *Fool in the Rain*.

I was intrigued. Who was Rusty, after all? Why was Harry asking him to talk with the team? And why were he and his coaches as glued to Rusty's words as any speaker I had ever seen?

I made sure all of the bags were spread out evenly, and with the rain coming down harder and harder, I stepped away to my car to check my cell phone.

I needed to know who I was working for and what this was all about.

CHAPTER 7
A LEGEND IN HIS OWN RIGHT

It didn't take long for me to find Rusty with a simple online search. Thirty-nine years in professional baseball. Seven former proteges who worked under Rusty also went on to be grounds crew chiefs for other professional franchises. I was working for a legend. I kept reading various articles about Rusty and it was clear he was widely respected as a leader, a mentor and an expert in his field.

"You have to complete the forms before you go," said the marketing intern. "What?" I replied, startled by his stealth approach to my cracked-open driver's side window. "Harry said don't leave until you complete your HR forms in the press box," he explained.

When I arrived at the press box atop the bleachers behind home plate, it was empty. Nobody was there and there were no forms for me to sign. The rain had slowed to a drizzle and the press box gave me a perfect view of Harry and Rusty talking outside the third-base dugout. I made my way down to the gate that led me onto the field near them. Harry saw me, turned back to Rusty with a firm handshake and slapped his back. He was fired up.

He walked toward me, smiling wide, and shouted an energetic "Jimbo! So good to have you on board!" He was already through the gate and halfway to his car as I reached ground level.

Rusty was in the dugout grabbing for his hat on one of the hooks behind the bench. I decided it was time to learn more about him and how his incredible career led him to Chinooks baseball, of all places.

Rusty said, "Well Jimmy, today is a washout, so why don't we start fresh tomorrow? I'll give you this binder that I put together for you so you can read through it before tomorrow. It'll give you a feel for how we will do things as a party of two."

"OK, thank you," I replied. "Rusty, I looked you up on my phone during the storm and your career in the big leagues was incredible. How did you end up in Mequon?"

I immediately realized I only knew Rusty for about 90 minutes before I asked a very personal question. "I'm sorry if I'm asking too much or if it's...please tell me to mind my own...." Rusty interrupted me: "Well, Jimmy, if you have a few minutes, I'll tell you. Sit down. No time like a rainout to get to know one another.

I could keep you all day with tales of my years working in the big leagues—all of the great players, managers and coaches who eat, drink and sleep baseball. I could tell you about the spiritual place that is a Major League Baseball ballpark and the chills you get every opening day. I could try to explain the feeling of witnessing a boy or girl who sees our green grass with their own eyes for the first time. I could also tell you how I was blessed to have a front row seat to our national pastime and to see how the game changed, and changed again. However, what I hope to share with you this summer is what impacted me the most, and that's the people. And how my relationships with many of them changed my life.

I believe great leaders must first be great followers, and what you may not have read about is my mentor, Charlie Keyes. Charlie taught me this most important lesson: that if you surround yourself with great people, you can all come together around a few shared values. The people and the values create a bond, and that team bond becomes unbreakable. That unbreakable bond becomes a culture more important than anything else.

When Charlie retired in Milwaukee in 1991, I was promoted. I did my best to advance Charlie's system and approach. Through the years, I've been fortunate that seven members of my staff have gone on to become grounds crew chiefs at other professional organizations. I'm proud of them and humbled that Charlie's system endures. So, how did I get to Mequon is the question, right?"

It was like he was reading my mind. "Yes," I said.

"Well, if our work is about the people and the relationships, then the people in your personal life should also be enjoying that with you; otherwise you have a career that's just built on sand and will collapse when adversity hits." Rusty's voice started to soften, and he became emotional.

"In my 39 years in the game, working on and later leading ground crews, my wife, Susan, was the love of my life and we shared it all together. We hosted events throughout the year for my team and their families. We had cookouts at our home each spring, summer picnics when the team was away on a road trip, and even an Oktoberfest each fall when the season ended.

Three years ago, Susan was diagnosed with a rare form of breast cancer. I took leave from work as we went to MD Anderson in Houston for some experimental trials. Despite countless efforts and many different treatments, we lost Susan 12 months ago.

My son, Patrick, daughter-in-law Kate, and three kids live in Mequon. After the services I came to stay with them for what I thought was going to be a few weeks. I went back to work but I couldn't continue with the same energy and passion I needed to be great at my job without Susan by my side.

With her gone I thought it was time to start a new chapter. Last summer Patrick and I would bring his kids—my grandkids—to some Chinooks games. Harry is such a baseball junkie he recognized me in the stands," Rusty chuckled.

Rusty started to tear up and continued with, "Harry wouldn't take no for an answer, so when Coach Delancey called him about you, Harry asked me if I would help out and here we are, my friend. Today marks the one-year anniversary of Susan's passing."

I didn't know what to say. Rusty was sort of crying, half smiling and shaking his head all at once. At that moment, exactly one year full of emotions came out. All of the firsts without his beloved Susan seemed to be running through his mind right there in the dugout. I didn't know what to say. I could hear my mom telling me to hug him, and so I did. Rusty wasn't expecting it, but he hugged me back.

As we processed his emotional moment, I realized how fortunate I was to be there with him one year to the day. It also dawned on me how clever Harry was to find a creative way for Rusty to be a part of the Chinooks family.

I broke the silence. "Hey, Rusty, as you know, I was supposed to be in that dugout when you talked with the team earlier. If I hadn't broken my wrist I would have been there, and yet, I wouldn't have been here with you now. Can you teach me what you learned from Charlie and what you taught to your teams? I want to be a leader; I want to be a part of great teams; and I know great teams have great relationships and a sustainable culture."

Rusty, still emotional in his own stoic Rusty way, simply replied with, "Good. Let's meet here tomorrow at 5:30 a.m."

CHAPTER 8
MY FAVORITE ENERGY DRINK

I remember walking to my car after our exchange, with an unbelievable feeling of gratitude. I stopped ruminating about my broken wrist and stopped feeling sorry for myself for a minute. I guess Coach D was right: feeling sorry for yourself is a worthless emotion.

As soon as I got into my vehicle, I typed the Bowmans' address into the GPS and called my dad from the car as I drove to their home. I couldn't wait to tell him about what just happened. He thought it was very cool and reminded me that this was the silver lining. He said, "Remember, Jimmy, when one door closes, even if it slams closed on your wrist, another door will open and it's up to you to walk through it. The attitude you take is a decision you make, and it's the most important decision you make every day. I'm proud of you, that you went to Wisconsin despite the cast on your wrist. Now look at the great opportunity you have—to learn from Rusty."

My dad has a knack for perspective when it matters most. It could be his humble upbringing, that his hardworking parents instilled strong values. He deserves a lot of credit, too. He took chances in life that required courage; he trusted his instincts. His street smarts were honed playing stickball growing up and later, in taverns he owned, he learned from an older generation the many unspoken rules of the restaurant business and life.

As we talked, I could feel his own excitement coming through the phone. He knew I was in this position because I didn't stop when I was given a setback. He had always taught me that a setback was just a setup for a comeback.

"Ok, Dad, I told the Bowmans I'd join them for dinner, so I gotta run," I said as we finished the call. I didn't sleep much that night. I was too excited from reading Rusty's training manual, and feeling grateful that I was still able to be part of a team and part of the game, albeit not on the field where I wanted to be.

I arrived at the Chinooks ballpark the next morning at 5:10. I thought I beat Rusty there until I saw his bike leaning up against the back of the third-base dugout.

Before he saw me, he must have heard my feet on the crushed gravel. "Morning, Jimmy."

"Good morning, Rusty," I replied.

"I take it you're not a regular member of the 5 a.m. Club?" I was not. The only time I could recall waking that early by choice was to play golf or to go bass fishing back home.

Rusty handed me my favorite energy drink. "I called Coach Delancey yesterday. He told me what you drink. I wasn't sure if you were a coffee drinker...yet," he said. Rusty had a kind of crooked smile that took up his entire face. His wrinkles were worn where years of smiles had passed.

"You and your teammates are fortunate to have him as your coach. I can tell he truly cares about you all. As we talked, his humility came right through and he was quick to highlight the work of his staff and the talented student-athletes he was coaching...like you.

"He also mentioned the word mission more than once. It was like he could give this morning's talk. You see, Charlie taught me many years ago to *push the tarp*.

"Charlie's recipe for great teams was communicated through the metaphor of the tarp. Simple as it may be, I think you can appreciate that simple isn't always easy.

"Charlie's three rules were:

1. We *all* show up.
2. We *all* push.
3. We *keep* pushing.

"As you think about those three rules, they translate into the three pillars of:

1. Service
2. Teamwork
3. Persistence

"This morning, we are going to talk about *service*."

"When we say we all show up to the tarp, we mean we all collectively serve the cause," Rusty began. I realized I had already experienced my first lesson without knowing it. I jumped in by saying, "That makes more sense now. When the storm rolled in yesterday, everyone showed up to push...including you, Harry, his coaches and even the marketing intern."

"That's right, Jimmy," Rusty replied. "The first element of great teams in the Push the Tarp system is that we all show up. By that, we mean we have a shared desire to serve a common cause, mission, goal or pursuit. We all agree at the outset that this value of service—of showing up each time—comes first, because you can't accomplish anything if you don't show up, and further, show up in service of something greater than oneself.

"To serve, we believe we have to live out three values and mesh them together:

1. Love
2. Humility
3. Mission-Driven Purpose

"The first is to love and care for those we lead and work with. If leaders exhibit a sense of genuine interest in who they are leading, it creates an environment where the team feels encouraged to show a similar level of care.

"Charlie wasn't energetic like Harry, for example. Leaders come in all shapes and sizes, from all backgrounds and in every role within an organization. Charlie's form of love was authentically his own. When I finished my first day working for him, he gave me a note that I keep in my wallet." Rusty pulled out the piece of paper, which was taped and folded several times. He handed it to me. It said:

"Rusty, we're glad to have you on our team. Please know I care and we care about you and we are grateful to have your two hands pushing the tarp with us. See you tomorrow. CK"

"Charlie was not a hugger or even a talker, for that matter, and yet from day one, he set the tone for me that I was cared for as we served together. I am a big believer that people don't care what you know until they know that you care, and Charlie let people know immediately and often that he cared."

"The second part of service is to be humble. That sense of love and care has to blend well with genuine humility...the desire to be part of something greater than oneself. Charlie would often say that you can't push by yourself. It's why it's the perfect metaphor to me. The tarp was our symbol, our reminder that greatness doesn't happen by yourself, so we approached our work with a humility that we are all parts of something special. Our specific roles on the team may be different and we are all equally respected and valued members of our unit."

I thought back to my high school basketball coach who would often say that we were too nice. And that we should stop being so humble.

"Rusty," I interjected, "I thought being humble was a sign of weakness or a lack of confidence."

"Another good point, Jimmy," he replied. "To be humble is not to be less confident. It's the reverse. It's to be so secure in your ability and your sense of self that you are willing to be a valued part of something rather than the only part. It's not thinking less of yourself: it is thinking of yourself less often—because you are focused on serving a greater cause."

Rusty was on a roll now. I had more questions but I didn't want to hijack his flow. He was rollin' like a great tarp push in mid-summer form.

"The third element of service is being mission-driven. If we approach our journey with a sense of love and genuine care for those we are working with, and we keep a keen sense that we are humble parts of something special and something bigger than us, then service is fortified and sustained by the collective mission.

"For you at school, that can be the mission of your team, athletics department or university. We believe great teams state their mission and keep it front and center to guide and inform them in their pursuits.

"For me, it was always to create an atmosphere where the organization, players and fans never worried about the state of the field. We were the stage-setters, the dream-makers, the team behind the team. We took pride in hiding in plain sight and then when the storms rolled in, we rolled out and we pushed the tarp. Shadow warriors, the Navy SEALs of our industry— there when it gets stormy, to do the work that nobody wants to do, but it is a necessary job if everyone else is to see the game.

"We did it with love. We humbly served so players could play and fans could enjoy the time with their friends and family. We never lost sight of our service-first, humble, mission-driven mentality. Our mission was simply: *to push the tarp in the sun and the rain so others can enjoy our national pastime.* When you walked into our bunker clubhouse under the stands, you would see a piece of white athletic tape above the door with **Push the Tarp** written in black marker. If you were on our team you needed to know what this meant at your core and if you didn't get it or couldn't embrace this mission, we found a way to compassionately coach you to find another place of employment outside of our team."

Rusty took his hat off and scratched his head like he probably did during the thousands of rain delays he had experienced. I can't say why, but it was awesome...like a window into a July thunderstorm in 1988.

He said a lot in that morning session but his mannerisms, as I have found with many great leaders, said almost as much. Most of all, I recall how emotionally connected he was to these parts of service.

As he scratched his head and I imagined the mid-summer rain delay, I envisioned Rusty smiling wide and looking out to the field. He was a look-you-in-the-eye kind of guy, so I noticed. He smiled that crooked smile and said quietly, "What's even more gratifying is that the seven former teammates we trained and worked with who lead big league crews today...they have that same white tape and black marker with **Push the Tarp** above their doorway like we did. Like Charlie first did. Our own lineage, and I have to say, it's really meaningful, you know?"

It was one of those questions you don't answer. Rather, you sit in the moment and be grateful. I was truly grateful and now increasingly committed to being about service, and to be on a team that believed in these elements of love, humility and being driven by a guiding mission.

"Let's put service in action, Jimmy," Rusty said. "We have a busy week ahead with the Chinooks. Harry scheduled doubleheaders on Saturday and Sunday and the storm system doesn't seem to be moving out any time soon. Here's what I want you to do this week: pay attention to examples of leaders and teams that exemplify service. You can pull from something you see at the grocery store, on the field here or elsewhere. It doesn't matter. The idea is to seek it out and to be aware of it when you find it. What do you see and what do you not see? Let's meet again next Monday at 5:15 a.m."

Rusty paused. "Any questions?" he asked.

I responded, "Do you want me to write it down or...?"

"Yes, good point. Thank you. You know, you're my first student, so you're going to make me a better teacher, too. Yes, write each example down in a notebook or journal. Also, the night before we meet, it would be helpful for you to do something I call 'The Well-Better-How.'

"Write down where you see service done well. For examples where you witnessed a form of service that could be improved, write what could be done Better and then, finally, write down How.

"I do this for myself every Sunday. It helps me reflect on my past week. We will discuss the power of reflection more in the third pillar of this framework. For now, start with observing service and reflecting on it with The Well-Better-How exercise in your journal."

"Thank you, Rusty," I replied.

He finished by saying something that has stayed with me all these years later. "Jimmy, one last point before we break. Our Push the Tarp motto is all about action. Charlie had a favorite Teddy Roosevelt quote. We found it taped in his center desk drawer after he retired.

"The quote reads: 'Get action. Do things; be sane; don't fritter away your time; create, act, take a place wherever you are and be somebody; get action.'

"You see, we can *talk* about service all we want, and yet, only action makes it happen."

The week after my first of three sessions with Rusty went fast. I found myself more grounded, more aware of how I was going about my day and much more aware of service happening around me. I journaled every evening, detailing examples of good and not-so-good service.

My favorite example that week was Harry. Aside from Rusty and me, Harry was the first at the ballpark each day. Coach D had shared Harry's morning routine with me before I left home. Harry was up around 5 a.m., performed a daily exercise routine he called sweat before screens, in which he exercised before looking at his phone, TV or laptop. He meditated, journaled and spent time with his family before he started his workday. He wanted to take the best care of himself first before he could serve others. He created his energy and Coach D told me his routine helped him lose over 100 pounds.

When Harry arrived at the ballpark, he would walk the perimeter of the field, looking for anything to throw out and keep the field in pristine shape. He then checked in with Rusty and me, and most days, he would rake home plate and the pitcher's mound before I could get to it on my to-do list.

Once the team arrived, Harry would organize the Chinooks' bags in a certain way in the dugout to create order. After he did this a few times, I would see some of the players take action and organize the bags. And after a week, the bags were all ordered as Harry had demonstrated.

The other thing Harry did that I thought was unique is he would call one player out by name during stretching and walk a lap of the field with him. This was his way of checking in with his players. How is the bed at your host family? Do you have the right cleats? What are you eating for breakfast? How are you staying in touch with your family? And then he would ask the player for a one-word focus for the next week. This was Harry's way to show the Chinooks that he cared for them. He was a servant leader if I ever saw one.

My personal foray into service came with the Bowmans. Meghan and Sally played softball. Compelled by Rusty's lesson on service, I volunteered to help Mr. Bowman coach his daughters. It was rewarding to assist and to see their joy playing the game. When I would get home from the ballpark, they would often be waiting to have a catch in the backyard and I did my best catching and throwing with one arm.

The start of the second week arrived with beautiful weather. The sunrise on Lake Michigan in June in Mequon might be the best of the year, often blended with a light fog that burns off in time for practice at 7:15 a.m.

For the second lesson, the fog and the sun shining through at 5:15 Monday morning was a perfect setting for Rusty to share pillar two with me.

"Good morning, Jimmy. I hope you had a great Sunday off. I'm excited to share our second pillar of Push the Tarp, which is *teamwork*. For this lesson, I thought we could walk the field and talk."

Rusty shared what he and his teams meant when they said *we all push*. "When we think about teamwork as our second pillar, we drill down to call out three elements that together form our ideal type of teamwork. These three are:

1. Connected teammates
2. Vulnerable teammates
3. Teammates who execute their role

"I want to share a story with you about one of my favorite teammates in all of my years in the big leagues. His name was Vinny. Vinny, who always called me *Cap*, was from Queens, like your folks. He followed a girl out to Milwaukee one summer and found a role on our crew. He didn't know a thing about our work, and that was OK. His essential skills and natural teamwork was a thing of beauty. I would normally ask our team to arrive at the ballpark by 7 a.m. While I was usually in by 5:15, Vinny was almost always the first teammate to join me in the clubhouse. He embraced all three pillars of our system and he really shined when it came to teamwork.

"Vinny had this engaging, hardworking quality that allowed him to challenge his teammates to meet him with the same level of effort. First though, and this is where I thought he was really special, he would kind of check in with everyone when they arrived.

"He would look them in the eye and see if they seemed present. If they were tired he would sometimes get them coffee or put on their favorite song. Other times, he had a gift to ask questions and listen and he would always rally the team if he thought someone needed to be heard, if someone was frustrated or if someone was excited and simply wanted to share something in their life.

"In short, Vinny connected through all types of verbal and non-verbal communication with his team and he fostered that type of environment among the team. After a while, teammates were connecting with each other on a deeper level and it created a sense of belonging. They brought their best selves to the team.

"This type of connected communication starts at the top. I couldn't shut down during Susan's illness and let Vinny be the only one in charge, and yet his openness made me even more willing to communicate about

Susan and our family than I had before Vinny arrived. Inspired by Vinny, I started Friday Forums once a month where I could give updates and as importantly, teammates could recognize others who were Pushing the Tarp in special ways.

"On weeks when we didn't have scheduled Forums, I would often send a Friday message about something on my mind that was a way for me to connect, to be vulnerable and to share other news.

"Great teams are made of a connected group of individuals who have a desire to engage with their teammates, colleagues, and co-workers.

"We were good at communicating before Vinny arrived. Charlie set a high standard and Vinny's arrival helped me and our team reach an even greater level of communication.

"If you don't genuinely connect, it's hard to know what your team is carrying, and therefore, how you can support them. Sometimes we would send someone home and sometimes work was a great distraction from other life dynamics.

"In each case, the interaction is different and the connected camaraderie of our unit allowed us to support each other in this meaningful way."

"This leads me to the next element of teamwork, which is vulnerability. This might not be one that leaders call out much, yet I think it is absolutely essential.

"Vulnerability to me is the courage to ask for help and the grace to offer it. It's a sense of trust that exists in healthy and high-performing teams. To be vulnerable is to risk not always looking perfect or what you or others might perceive as great. And the magic happens when you're in that uncomfortable space. That is where personal and team growth can occur.

"I realized Vinny was very comfortable being vulnerable. One day, I asked him about that: 'Vinny, how did you get like this?' He stared back, not knowing what I meant completely. 'Like what, Cap?'

"You come early, you check in with your teammates and you create a trusted space. That's all impressive. However, who taught you to keep learning and growing and asking questions with little regard to whether the questions sound silly or obvious?"

Rusty enjoyed telling this story. "Vinny stepped back and said, 'That's easy, Cap: Lou Piniella!'

"'Lou Piniella?' I replied. 'Well,' Vinny explained further, 'truthfully, my dad. He was and still is a great fan of the Yankees. Mantle was his boyhood idol and he was partial to Thurman Munson and Mickey Rivers on those great Yankees teams of the late '70s. One day, though, when I was in high school, we were arguing about something and my dad said, 'You'll never hit the curveball if you worry about how you look!'

"It disarmed me and rather than being frustrated or mad, I became curious. He said, 'You think Lou Piniella cares how he looks when he hits the curveball? He wants to compete, he wants to win...and to be a great teammate and to do that, sometimes you have to hit the curveball off your front foot and send it to the opposite field. I can still picture my dad mimicking Sweet Lou's lean as he served that ball into the outfield.'

'From that day on, Cap, I was less concerned with being cool or asking the safe questions. My dad helped me learn that if we want to grow and learn and be a great teammate—maybe one day be a leader of a great team—we have to be willing to get comfortable being uncomfortable.'

Rusty stopped as we were almost to the right field foul pole. "Vinny was and still is my most impressive protege. He never intentionally set out to be vulnerable. He was blessed to grow up in a house that encouraged it, fostered it and talked about it in their own, Lou Piniella story, way."

We stood at the right field foul pole for a few minutes. The tarp had been resting on the right field foul line fence since the storm the previous week. Rusty then continued, "Jimmy, we talked about being connected and vulnerable. The third part of great teams is to embrace your role. We call this *executing* your role and equally important, respecting the roles of your teammates. I'll explain the nuance of this element by telling you the story of Big John."

Before Rusty started in on Big John, I asked him, "You say We All Push and then you say we have to Execute our Roles. Aren't those in conflict with one another?"

"Great question, Jimmy, great question. Simple answer is no. Both are true and your question is the perfect segue to Big John. Let me explain.

"Big John was from Davenport, Iowa. A little different than Long Island, like you, and Queens, like Vinny. He and I started the same day and learned from Charlie. He didn't say much, so when he did, everyone listened. Charlie knew John's uncle and his uncle sent John up to Milwaukee the same spring I started. While he was not a talker, he was not cold or mean spirited. His handshake was like a death grip. If you didn't get into the pocket, your fingers wouldn't soon forgive you. He was quiet, he liked to have lunch by himself and you would find him reading classic books or works by Plato, Dickens or Emerson rather than playing cards with our crew.

"When we started, Charlie explained Push the Tarp— that we all show up, that we all push and that we keep pushing. It was Charlie's 1980s version of onboarding and it was clear to both of us. Big John was 6'5" and strong. God gave him his height, his parents gave him his work ethic and the farm gave him his build. Big John was classic farm-boy strong.

"Charlie found in me someone he could develop to help him interact with management, to help hire and onboard new teammates and to deal with vendors on pricing, purchasing and servicing our equipment.

"Big John was excellent with the equipment, a natural in all things grass and dirt and clay. He could feel a summer storm in Madison well before it rolled into Milwaukee. Our roles were different and equally important. We trusted Charlie to put us in the right roles and to develop us, and it was up to us to embrace these roles and work hard to master the skills each role required. For our team to succeed, I had to execute my role and respect the role that Charlie had given Big John, and vice versa.

"One thing never changed, however: that we all pushed. When it was time to get behind the tarp in those years when Big John and I were working for the great Charlie Keyes, you could find Big John in the center. I was usually on one end because I was good at getting a quick grip of a corner once it was off the roll. When we had new teammates Big John was fond of belting out early in the roll, 'It's OK, I got it! It will roll itself. Just put your hands on it. I got it!'

"Ahhh, we all push!" I said.

"'That's right," Rusty replied. 'Simple right?' But as Charlie often said: 'Simple ain't easy.'

"When your head hits the pillow at night, you take the pillow test. You ask yourself, *what did I do well today?* and reflect on what you could have done differently or better. Every night our goal is to pass the pillow test by saying, *I'm glad I did and not just I wish I had.*

"In a similar way, Big John was telling our new teammates, 'I might be twice your size and much stronger, but we are all here to Push the Tarp. We execute our roles and one common thread is that when we show up, we all push.'"

"Why does that matter?" I asked. I was a little confused.

"Why does what matter, Jim?" Rusty asked.

"I get the part about distinct roles based on strengths and personalities, but why would Big John care about his teammates not pushing?" I asked.

"Ok, I see. Let me try and say it this way," Rusty said. "Practically speaking, Big John couldn't push the tarp on his own, and so it would take a group of us to do it with him. We could have simply designated the 10 strongest teammates to push and leave the other 10 or so to perform other roles.

"However, when we all work together as best as we can, the tarp gets lighter and the stronger colleagues don't become resentful of the teammates who aren't next to them. The teammates who are not naturally as strong also became more motivated to be more physically fit so they can be even more helpful.

"Last, an unspoken bond was also formed when we all pushed as best we could. When you think back to some of your best moments on teams, it could be the bus rides, the time stretching in the outfield before practice or your off-season workout sessions early in the mornings, those moments pull you closer as a team.

"Great teams are made up of bonds formed by respecting the specific, individual roles and common, entire-team rituals. For us, as you now well know, our all-team ritual was the tarp.

"What Big John was saying, ultimately, is that only you can tell if you are truly pushing to your best. It didn't matter if you couldn't push like Big John—frankly nobody could. It is everything, however, if you don't push your best for your teammate standing to your right and left. So we execute our roles as best we can and we come together to execute our one common ritual.

"Does that answer your question? Because it was a good one." Rusty inquired as he turned toward me.

"Yes, it does." I replied. "I guess executing your role is customized to you at that place in time, and yet great teams embrace a common ritual to develop a common bond."

Rusty liked that. "Well said, Jimmy." He continued, "Let's stop here on teamwork. Take this week and now in addition to journaling on service, observe where you see great examples of teamwork as in our definition.

For teamwork, specifically keep an eye on the Chinooks. They have three home games this week and it will be a good case study. Next Monday, let's meet again at 5:15 a.m. for our final session on the third element of our system: *persistence.*"

CHAPTER 17
THE CHINOOKS

The week between my teamwork and persistence session was fantastic. The Chinooks had three home games: one each on Tuesday, Wednesday and Friday. They had away games over the weekend, which allowed me to help the Bowmans' 5th grade softball team.

For teamwork, Rusty asked me to add the Well-Better-How (WBH) exercise to my journal. He asked me to focus this WBH on the Chinooks teamwork.

After watching them from the left field bullpen over the three-game homestand, I witnessed great teamwork and clear areas for improvement. My WBH looked like this:

Well:

- Chinooks are connected. They communicate, they act and interact well with each other.

- Harry cultivates pregame rituals that help foster connection and consistency.

- Each player seemed focused on executing their given roles for each game.

Better:

- Phillips mis-played two balls in left field due to the bright sun and he did not have sunglasses on.

- No teammates or coaches offered help when McDonald struck out three times in three at bats.

- Smith struggled at catcher when balls were pitched in the dirt. Too many base runners advanced on past balls.

How:

- Phillips could ask coaches for help and talk more with Maxwell in centerfield to let him know he's struggling with the sun and that he may need Maxwell to cover more ground in the left-center field gap.

- McDonald seems lost at plate with breaking balls and seems to have lost his confidence. Also, not asking for help similar to Phillips.

- Teammates could offer to help others who are struggling like Vinny did on Rusty's team.

This was my first WBH, so my weekly routine improved. When I shared this via text with Rusty on Saturday, I also commented that Harry and his coaches were not hands-on at all. They set a positive tone in pregame and were upbeat but they didn't do anything in the games other than change the lineup.

Rusty texted me back: "I told them not to." When I asked him why, he said, "I wanted Harry, his staff and you to see the positive points and where the team could improve. If the coaches jumped in on giving help and encouraging questions, it wouldn't be this clear. Harry and his staff are going to have their own Well-Better-How session on Monday with the team around being more vulnerable."

As scheduled, I arrived at 5:15 the following Monday to learn about persistence.

It was another crisp, late-June morning and I noticed that Rusty's bike was not leaning up against the back of the third-base dugout like usual.

I walked into the dugout and saw a note from Rusty on the cork board that posted the batting lineups:

"Jimmy: I'll be back at 6:15 a.m. Please get started on the list (attached to this note) and we will discuss persistence when I'm back."

I got started on Rusty's list. It included things like getting the music set up for practice, putting up the American flag and Wisconsin state flag, and dragging the infield dirt with the tractor. I also opened the storage closets so the team could set up for batting practice when they arrived at 7:15.

The quiet hour alone allowed me to reflect on my time in Wisconsin so far. How blessed I was that despite a broken wrist, I was learning from Rusty about *a proven mindset that fosters authentic leaders and great teams*.

As I worked my way through Rusty's list, it made sense to start with service—to create a foundation of love and care, an approach of humility and to connect to a mission larger than ourselves. It also makes sense that great service is enhanced by teams who are connected, who execute their roles and who are vulnerable to ask questions and trust their teammates to offer ways they can help.

I was curious how persistence would complement service and teamwork. I finished Rusty's assigned work with 10 minutes to spare and in the quiet of the morning, I sat in the dugout with my notebook that I used to keep notes from Rusty's sessions. I also used it for my journal to capture examples of service (good and bad) as well as my teamwork WBH from last week's Chinooks games.

With a few minutes before Rusty was to arrive, I found myself writing in my journal. As I think back now, it was the day I started my daily practice of journaling—putting on paper what was in my head so I could create more clarity, present-moment focus and mindfulness.

I recall Coach Delancey talking about his morning journal sessions. He would say it helped him get his thoughts out and he would often meditate for 10 minutes prior by just sitting, focusing on his breath in a very simple way. It would center him for the day ahead. Coach D was a morning person.

I haven't missed many days journaling since that morning alone in the dugout, and I have rarely, if ever, missed two days in a row. I try hard not to miss two days in a row because one of the few things I remember from psychology class is how if you miss two days in a row of a habit, that causes a streak and often leads to a dramatic decrease in that behavior. And, like Coach D, I have added 10 minutes of meditation before each journaling session.

CHAPTER 19
PERSISTENCE

I heard Rusty's bike roll up on the crushed gravel as I journaled. He turned into the dugout and seemed happy to see me using my notebook.

"Morning, Jimmy. Good work with the list. Thank you. It's also great to see you using your notebook. I've used a notebook or journal for many years after watching Charlie meticulously plan his days in his planner. One thing I added to my daily journal session is to set up my day the night before.

"Charlie strongly suggested we read Dale Carnegie's books when we joined the team. Some teammates didn't but Big John devoured them and I still read them once a year.

"One part that resonated with me in *How to Stop Worrying and Start Living* is "Just for Today." It's about being intentional with your day and having a plan. As I get ready for bed each night, I write down a few things I plan to do the next day. I also review my calendar and try to schedule every task, meeting and event. These days I use my Google calendar.

"Carnegie's books help me with many things, from anxiety to organization, and also with what we will discuss this morning: persistence.

"Charlie had Just for Today framed on his office wall.

"In many ways it is a recipe for persistence and Charlie would always remind us to live, as Carnegie wrote, *in day-tight compartments*. To Charlie, me, Big John and all the teammates who have since adopted our Push the Tarp system, persistence comes down to:

1. Staying **Present**
2. Being **Passionate**
3. Daily **Practice**

"These are our three P's of persistence. When we say persistence, it is about the mindset that we keep pushing the tarp. Now, that can take on many forms in life. It applies to whatever you are doing personally and professionally.

"For the teams I led in Milwaukee, it meant that our work is a constant pursuit. I liked to call this *staying in the pocket of our pursuits*. The attitude that the journey we are on, the journey we choose, is the destination.

"The first P is being Present. All we have is this moment. I always say that we stay present to make each moment count. It's a mindset to not count the days but make the days count.

"Coach D was telling me how he thinks you've been very distracted this season and maybe overthinking your past and being anxious about outcomes. Optimal performance comes from being where your feet are and living, loving and competing in the moment."

I admitted, "I think he's right. I feel like I don't have a solid approach, and I get caught in endless loops of thought about the past and future."

"Good!" Rusty replied. "To be present, we need an approach, consistent routines and habits that help us be and stay as present as possible. If we have routines and habits, they become an effective process for us to stay in the moment and best adjust to the curveballs that come our way each day—literally and figuratively.

"For our teams, we had a checklist of sequential tasks that started each day. They were up on the wall and they were consistent. Your list this morning was a mico-version of our morning routine. A morning routine for us was set each workday. Any adjustments to it needed to be made by the end of the day before, so we avoided hurrying or confusion.

"Once we all punched through our roles on the morning routine and checklist, we gathered in the circle for any updates from me that morning. If I couldn't be there, I would have Vinny or another teammate share updates.

"We called this 'Horizons' and then we had 30 minutes of quiet break for each teammate to set their personal intentions for their day in the habit or habits they thought were most effective for them.

"For me, I meditated for 10 minutes, journaled and then checked through my written mind map (also in my journal) to-do list for the day ahead. I found this kept me present and focused.

"Other teammates did the same or used the time to pray or read. Some listened to music on headphones, stretched or did yoga because they felt it prepared them for the day ahead.

"Charlie would read the Bible because it fueled his faith and gave him perspective. It doesn't matter much what routine you create; it matters more that you have one you can repeat each day to help you stay present and get started. It's the start that stops most people from being great.

"In the afternoon, we added a session of play or games to keep us present. I often played ping pong, other teammates played cards and you can imagine Big John with his nose in his books."

I interrupted: "Did Big John never play or interact with you guys? That seems very antisocial."

Rusty answered, "I wouldn't call it antisocial. He was using his time in the way he thought best for him. When we were working together, Big John was always connected, trustworthy, open to feedback and willing to help—even though he had fun ribbing the newbies on their first roll.

"All that said, Jimmy, there was one game we could get Big John to play, and that was chess.

"One day, Vinny and another teammate were playing chess on a board I brought in as a gift. My son taught me how to play and I liked the competitiveness and strategic thinking that's required. I kept seeing Big

John look up from his book. I quietly told Vinny to invite Big John next and after some encouragement, he obliged. Turns out it was the nighttime family entertainment at his farm growing up in Davenport.

"Big John didn't lose much, either! He was quite the competitor. This form of play gave us a different way to be present together that matched our morning quiet. It helped the more extroverted teammates get some present energy in the afternoon and the more introverted could enjoy having a quieter start to their day—all within the framework of a very productive day pushing the tarp.

"When we can be present, we are not ruminating on past mistakes or feeling anxious about the future. We are planful, we are organized and we are making each moment count to the best of our ability.

"I mentioned energy, which brings me to the second P: Passion."

CHAPTER 20
PASSION

"When we talk of passion, we mean an authentic energy—that you are interested in your work and the people you are working with. Commencement speakers talk about 'following your passions' as a key to a lifetime of happiness. That might be the case for some people but it can also be a recipe for disaster if we are only focused on following a passion.

"Others have suggested to not follow your passions and to focus more on your skills. I think this approach can also be flawed. In our approach, passion is a critical component of persistence because it serves as a reminder when things get tough—why you are in your pursuit and doing what you do. If we can stay present with routines, habits and a smart process, passion is the genuine energy that can fuel us when things get hard. And things will get hard.

"Every grounds crew has a routine and mode of operation of some sort. I believe our culture allowed us to function at a high level in the sun and the rain...on the cold spring days and in the heat of the summer. Our genuine passion to be part of a professional grounds crew carried us on those summer days when our friends and families were at a cookout, a lake or a golf course. Our passion to be the best crew in the game helped us through the hardest, most frustrating moments.

"I learned this one element of passion from Charlie. He would say, the first moments when you wake up each day are often the most honest seconds of your day. I believe that, too. That is when you realize whether you are feeding your passion or stifling it.

"Are you serving your passions and your dreams, and having the courage to pursue them? Passion is the glue of persistence. It binds your present focus and plan with the third element of persistence: *practice*."

"One of my favorite quotes is often attributed to Aristotle: 'You are what you repeatedly do. Excellence, then, is a habit.'"

"Our passion binds our ability to stay present with our routines and habits and connects it to our ability to practice our work again and again and again.

"Persistence is a beautiful thing to those committed to being great at whatever they pursue. It's my favorite pillar of Push the Tarp and the ability of one to put the effort into honing their skills over time and in spite of any and all obstacles.

"Practice is about repeated action. It allows you to make the most of your present moments—moments that you pursue with energy and enthusiasm (passion). Your drive to keep practicing makes the routine moments your path toward mastery.

"I practiced the things I was good at. I enjoyed learning from Charlie and connecting with our teammates. I learned more from Big John over the years, too, and we both helped each other practice in each other's areas of expertise."

By now, the team was arriving. Harry jumped in to let us know we were going to make up a rain delay from a week ago at 6:00 this evening.

"Ok, Jimmy," Rusty said, "let's stop here for now and wrap up persistence tomorrow morning with one of my favorite colleagues over my 39 years.

"After practice wraps, let's set up the field for pregame batting practice and I'll see you back here at 4 p.m."

The team went through a shortened practice, because they were playing later that night. I reviewed the three P's of persistence as I finished a few tasks and re-organized the first-base storage closet.

THE 3 P's OF PERSISTENCE

1. Present
2. Passionate
3. Practice

As I thought of my family and friends, teammates and classmates, many people came to mind who modeled at least one of these elements very well. My maternal grandmother was very faithful and it gave her a strong presence in each moment. She went through so much of life feeling blessed each day. She also gardened and baked and knitted, in addition to her career that gave her the habit of staying present through action and meaningful work and play.

One of my dad's heroes on and off the baseball diamond was Jackie Robinson. Jackie is legendary for breaking the color barrier as the first black professional baseball player. His stoic demeanor and poise in the face of racism from spectators, other teams and even members of his own team made him an inspiring example of turning the other cheek and rising above hatred and injustice.

In addition to all of this, Jackie's skill was remarkable. My dad raised me on stories about Jackie and the reckless abandon and relentless energy with which he played. He displayed a passion that was both beautifully graceful and competitively violent all at once.

His passionate energy still comes through on any footage you can find of him racing along the bases or diving for the ball as he played second base.

Along with his calmness and poise, his trailblazing courage and his grit carried him through as one of our most heroic and persistent Americans of all time.

I also thought of my best friend growing up. He was a talented athlete but his commitment to consistent practice allowed him to separate from many of us over time as he mastered any sport or activity from ping pong to basketball to soccer.

I was excited for Rusty's next story in the morning. First, though, was the makeup game at 6 p.m.

It was hard to believe I had been with the Chinooks for almost a month. I had two weeks left before I returned home to have my cast removed and to begin my painful rehab. Funny, I remember thinking to myself, *Good!* I guess Coach D, Harry and Rusty were starting to rub off on me.

I returned to the dugout at 4 p.m. and started my pregame tasks. It was a picture-perfect late afternoon, a great night for a game. The Bowmans were coming, too, and Meghan and Sally were going to be bat girls.

I saw Rusty talking with Harry and I was enjoying the new batting practice mixtape. It was one feel-good song after another and the music, the weather, the sound of the wood bats crackling during batting practice was its own melody that made me very happy to be there right then.

I still remember the first six songs:
1. "It's a Great Day to be Alive" - Travis Tritt
2. "Same Boat" - Zac Brown Band
3. "Walk of Life" - Dire Straits
4. "Burning Down the House" - Talking Heads
5. "Washing Dishes" - Jack Johnson
6. "Walking in Memphis" - Marc Cohn

My guess was that Harry had his hand in a few of the songs. He was always full of energy and batting practice and pregame was especially his element. His smile was wide as he fist-bumped anyone near him; he was excited for the upcoming chance to compete and he set a great example of serving the great game of baseball that he cherished.

Harry was an energy giver and my dad always told me that it was better to be an energy giver than an energy taker. I think Big John would have wanted to have him next to him any day.

I completed my pregame responsibilities and was waiting on an empty baseball bucket as I watched for the Bowmans to arrive so I could bring Meghan and Sally down to the dugout for their bat girl experience.

That's when I saw a woman get out of her car. She was about 50 feet from the first base dugout when she saw Rusty standing on the chain link fence and yelled his name in delight: "Rusty!"

He turned and came alive as they greeted each other with a big hug. Rusty saw me and immediately called my name. "Jimmy, come over here. I want to introduce you to one of my dear friends."

I hustled over and Rusty said, "Jimmy, this is Louise, the general manager of Milwaukee. She's the first woman to become a professional baseball GM and the person I was planning on talking about tomorrow morning to bring to life our third pillar of persistence."

Louise greeted me warmly as she shook my hand. "Jimmy, it's so nice to meet you. Sounds like Rusty might be sharing Push the Tarp with you, am I correct?"

I replied by saying, "He is, and so far we've covered service and teamwork and Rusty was sharing persistence this morning."

Rusty jumped in and said, "Louise, what is the GM of Milwaukee doing at a Chinooks game?"

Louise said, "I like to sit in on occasional scouting department meetings and they're even easier to join now with the virtual option. This time of year our scouts are everywhere and our area scout, Danny, who wanted to see a few Chinooks players, had a family emergency. Before they could pivot to another plan, I offered my services. Once a scout always a scout, and I thought it would be a great way to serve, to help our team and to surprise you, so here I am!"

Rusty's eyes grew wide. "Louise, how about you lean in one step further and stay after the game to talk with the Chinooks? They could really benefit from hearing your story. I know Harry and his staff would be all for it and the players and Jimmy here, who is nursing a broken wrist, would be greatly impacted to learn about your persistence in your journey.

"We won't post anything on social media or take any pictures, so you wouldn't get flooded with requests— any more than you already do, that is—and I'll buy you dinner after."

Louise was reluctant. She was busy, she was incredibly humble and yet, she couldn't turn down her old friend. You could see their mutual respect and admiration.

"Only for you, Rusty," Louise responded.

"Fantastic! I'll tell Harry." Rusty came alive again, like the first day we met when we were standing next to the tarp.

As Rusty went to share this special post-game talk with Harry, two kids ran up to me from behind and hugged me. Louise beamed again (she had a smile you didn't forget) and said, "Well, who is this?"

"Hi, I'm Meghan and this is my little sister, Sally. We are the bat girls tonight!" Meghan exclaimed.

"It's nice to meet you both. I'm Louise, a new friend of Jimmy's. After your work is done tonight, maybe you can join me as my guests when I talk with the team."

Louise looked at me and said, "Jimmy, if it's OK with Meghan and Sally's folks, it would mean a lot to me if they listened in on my message to the guys."

It was a moment I will never forget. There I was, standing in Mequon, Wisconsin, with the GM of Milwaukee, along with pre-teens Meghan and Sally. Louise was not only going to share her story after the game, she was going to scout the game first and then bring the girls along to join me for this impromptu post-game talk.

It's amazing what happens when you say yes to opportunities. You meet people you never would have met, and you have the chance to learn from them that wouldn't have come your way if you hadn't leaned in— if you hadn't shown up, pushed and kept pushing.

CHAPTER 23
GOOD!

The Chinooks won that night in dramatic fashion. Johnson carried a no-hitter through six innings only to give up two runs in the top of the seventh before Harry made a pitching change.

The Chinooks responded in the bottom half of that inning with three runs to take a one-run lead by none other than McDonald with a three-run double to right center field. The joy of his teammates could not be contained as they shouted "GOOD!" at him from the top step of the dugout. It was a running team joke with Harry because he said "Good!" all the time.

McDonald had slumped most of the season and Harry stuck with him in a key moment with the bases loaded. From my seat in the right field bullpen, I could see the assistant coaches fist-bump Harry for leaving Mac at bat and I could tell Harry was proud of Mac's resolve to keep practicing in between games with passion and to be present in the moment.

If that wasn't enough, the game ended with another feel-good team story. The Chinooks hustled out to the field with great enthusiasm after Mac's inspiring three-run double, needing only three outs to win that Monday night makeup game.

The Racine Generals, however, were a scrappy team in their own right and despite retiring the first two batters, they worked a walk and an infield hit to put two runners on and the tie run at second base. The next batter already had three hits and crisply lined the first pitch to left field. Phillips, who had struggled the previous week in left field, charged the ball, fielded it clean on two hops and made a great throw to Smith at home plate. (Smith had his own problems with past balls lately, too).

The runner was out at home plate and the Chinooks won the game. I'll never forget Maxwell hugging Phillips as the Chinooks stormed the field in excitement. For a Monday night makeup (or any game, for that matter), it was as good as it gets.

The Chinooks were becoming a true team and it was apparent they had bought in on the elements of Push the Tarp. They were playing for one another, playing for those in attendance and even playing for the bat girls, Meghan and Sally, who would one day be entertaining their own fans.

They were connected teammates, unafraid to ask for help or to give it. They were pumped for their teammates' success and they never quit. They also played in the moment with passion and conviction, at peace with whatever the outcome was because they were playing together as best they could and had become laser focused on this process.

As they celebrated a hard-fought team win, Harry brought them all together. They each took one knee in a circle in front of the third-base dugout. Harry gave out two game balls that night, one to Mac and one to Phillips. Phillips flipped his ball to Smith who caught the throw and made the tag to end the game. Phillips said he wanted Smith to have it and Harry laughed while everyone hollered: "GOOOOOOOOOD!"

It was a perfect way to lead into the message from Louise.

The celebration in front of the dugout continued with the players' orchestrated custom and specific individual handshakes. I received the OK from the Bowmans to let Meghan and Sally stay for Louise's talk. I also took the opportunity to introduce the family to Rusty.

Rusty said, "Thank you for hosting Jimmy. Without your hospitality, I would have never had the great pleasure to meet him." Mr. Bowman replied that it was their pleasure and remarked, "It's clear to us you have made a great impact on Jimmy in a very short time. We expected him to be on his smart phone all the time and stay mostly in our spare bedroom. Instead, he's helping in the kitchen and plays outside with me and the girls, practicing softball with us whenever he can."

Mr. and Mrs. Bowman went off to get ice cream for the girls while Rusty and I walked Meghan and Sally over to the dugout where Harry was getting the victorious Chinooks to settle down for a great nightcap of a gathering with Louise.

"OK, fellas," Harry said with his booming voice. "After a great team win, we have a special treat for our entire organization. Tonight you entertained the crowd with a game that embodies what we have been talking about with Rusty this season.

"We pushed the tarp in all three ways: we served each other, we did it together, and we stayed in the pocket of our pursuit...and we kept pushing when the Generals gave us all they could.

"When we talk about service, we also talk about serving a mission. For us, that has meant serving the great game of baseball and honoring everyone who graces us in the stands. Well, tonight we were blessed to have someone in the stands who has probably watched even more baseball than Rusty in her life.

Louise is the GM of Milwaukee and she was here tonight to help out a member of their scouting department who had a family emergency. Rusty and Louise are longtime friends, so I'll let Rusty say a few words and introduce Louise."

Rusty stepped over from where I was sitting with Meghan and Sally, and spoke. "Thank you, Harry. Great win tonight, guys. I'm proud of each one of you for playing a role in a complete team win.

"I'm also thrilled that my dear friend Louise surprised me tonight to scout you and the Generals. In my 39 years on a professional grounds crew and in life, I don't know if I've been around a better leader. I asked Louise to share her story with you, as I think you can learn from her path. It's an inspiring journey with many simple and profound lessons. Please give a warm Chinooks welcome to Louise."

"Well, thank you, Rusty," Louise began. "And good evening guys. Thanks to Harry, as well, for letting me crash your post-game celebration. I'm reluctant to impose on you after a great win and also grateful to be with you to share a little of my story. Rusty and I go way back, so it's impossible for me to say no to a request from a loyal friend.

"I could save you some time by telling you to Google me and check out a few interviews I've done in the last four years. I was blessed that the Milwaukee ownership believed in me enough four years ago to name me as the general manager of the organization, which at the time made me the first woman to serve in this role for a professional big league club. I'm glad to say now I'm one of three woman in this role.

"So for tonight, I'll share my story in maybe a different way and I'll challenge you to ask me some questions within the framework that you've all been learning from good ol' Rusty over here."

Rusty gave a subtle thumbs up, showing his approval of Louise's spontaneous idea.

"I'll start by saying I'm an only child born to two great parents. My mom was a nurse at our local hospital and my dad had a delivery route for Wise Potato Chips. He was also a baseball umpire in the evenings and on weekends.

"Growing up, I played any kind of sport I could, including soccer, basketball, and softball: I loved to compete. I tagged along with my dad whenever I was allowed, to watch him umpire, and that's how I became obsessed with our game of baseball.

"I enjoyed being at the ballpark, seeing how different players approached the game, the wide range of pitching styles, and that there was no clock on the game except for Mother Nature.

"My father was also quite a character at the baseball field. His signature way to eject a player from the game after the appropriate amount of warnings was to lean over to him and whisper, "Please tell your coach you are ejected from this game." He would walk into dugouts and drink from their water coolers, he would give teams a list of his favorite songs in case he returned, and he had a passion for the game. He was also a great technical umpire.

"As I got older I would start to scout one team each night in a notebook. He also started to umpire high school games and later, elite summer league games like tonight and then local college games.

When I was in high school, my dad was invited to join a minor league umpire school in Arizona. He and my mom talked about it for two weeks, agonizing over this prospect to pursue his dream of one day being a big league umpire. My mom was nervous about his being away but she was also very supportive. It was his decision and she agreed that she would make it work.

"In the end, my dad said no. He didn't want to leave us, he said, yet I think he let his fear of failure stop him. In this case, he let fear stop him from his dream of being a professional umpire.

"He returned to his day job of delivering chips to local delis and convenience stores throughout the suburbs of Chicago. He kept umpiring games throughout greater Chicagoland and my mom continued to serve as an excellent nurse.

"What I noticed in the year or so after was that he became more distracted at home and less energetic at ballgames, and he even said no to some umpire opportunities that he would normally have pounced on.

"I noticed all of this then, when I was in 8th grade, but when I think of it now, I realize that my dad stopped pushing the day when he said no to his dream.

"My first of three pieces of advice for you tonight is: one way or another, keep pushing your tarp in life.

"As my parents moved forward from my dad's decision, I was starting high school. I was an average athlete who always strived to be a great teammate. On my high school softball team, I was a reserve infielder. I tried to be the teammate who was first to help warm up the pitcher between innings, or to warm up with an outfielder.

"I was the teammate who threw the ball to the first baseman and center fielder when they returned to the dugout so they had a ball in their glove to warm up with when they ran back out for the next inning.

"All those days in the stands watching my dad umpire games also helped me become an unofficial coach. I found myself sharing tendencies with my coach and anticipated bunts and steals before they happened.

"Another thing occurred as I started 9th grade. I fell in love with learning. I naturally excelled in math and was blessed with classmates and teachers who created a wonderful community where we supported and challenged each other.

"I also became more interested in writing. My 9th grade teacher was my 7th grade teacher who moved up to 9th grade the same year I entered high school.

"Dr. D'Angelis helped me gain confidence in a subject in which I had much room for improvement. He was kind, tough, and very smart, and he taught us that writing should start with a consistent, simple structure. Similar to how you guys practice the basics of throwing, fielding and hitting every practice, right?"

Heads nodded. The guys were locked in and even Sally and Meghan were wide-eyed, like they were seeing into their future.

Louise was a gifted speaker. She was humble and engaging, with the special blend great leaders possess of high-level skill and inspiring energy.

"I tell you all about my academics because it was the foundation to my growth. I became so curious and eager to take on more in the classroom that it gave me confidence to try more in the sports I played.

"As high school progressed, it was clear I wasn't a college athlete. I was, however, admitted to my dream school, Stanford University—one of the places my best friend, Molly, was being recruited to play softball. In the end, after an intense recruiting period, she decided on Stanford, like me.

"Her coach heard about me and asked if I would consider serving as the team manager. Without hesitation, I agreed.

"In my role as manager, I did a little bit of everything. I also kept up my practice of scouting reports in between my studies and managerial duties. I enjoyed breaking down game film and assessing the talents of gifted athletes.

"As my college years continued, I made a name for myself on campus, most especially with the baseball coaches. They would see me at their games and knew that I kept a separate journal for baseball game scouts.

"I always say to *run your race*. It might be cliché, but when everyone was on spring break, I would be with softball or baseball somewhere. And if I wasn't, at night or in the early morning hours, I would be organizing my journals and breaking down game films.

"When it comes to being persistent, you have to be lost in the moment and have the courage of your convictions. You can't think about how long it will take. My mom was fond of saying, 'A watched pot never boils.' Immerse yourself in your passion fueled process and not how long until what you are doing will pay off; and remember that things built to last are not built fast.

"Have the passion to pursue it because it is something that brings you joy and something that, ultimately, you want to become great at doing over time."

"When I graduated from Stanford I was eager to break into professional baseball. I wanted to be a scout. I was committed, having learned from my dad a lesson in pursuing a dream, and I was passionate enough to do whatever it takes.

"I finally secured an interview with a scouting director for the Brooklyn Cyclones, Scott Collins. Scott asked where I was calling from and I said Palo Alto, California, as I had yet to move out of my off-campus apartment. I shared that I was planning to move to New York City that summer and he said to call him when I got to town.

"That was 2:14 p.m. in Palo Alto on May 22. I called him three days later from a motel along the Belt Parkway in Brooklyn. He thought I was kidding and when he realized I wasn't, he agreed to meet.

"All I wanted was a chance, and Mr. Collins gave me that. What followed was a 15-year journey through minor league baseball that I will not bore you with.

"I bounced from coast to coast, league to league, and thought of quitting almost daily for the first few years. After that I only contemplated giving up occasionally, and now I can't imagine any other path.

"Almost 10 years ago, I got a big break. I was hired by Milwaukee as a scout and have never looked back. Years of hard work paid off, years of preparation met an opportunity—and when opportunity knocks, you answer the door.

"I give credit to the entire Milwaukee front office. They didn't treat me or any of the scouts as only that. We were being taught how to be leaders, to be front office executives and to be part of a great team.

"I'll leave you with this last story. My mentor in Milwaukee is Jay Johnston. I replaced him as GM four years ago. One day in July he stopped at my cubicle and asked me to talk in front of a coaching convention in one week. I said yes, confidently, as he walked off. Then I panicked.

"I was learning a lot in the front office and I was confident in my skills as a judge of talent from my years as a scout. One thing I had not done at all was speak in public, and if I'm being honest, it scared me to death.

"I went for a walk in the underbelly of the stadium. I had never been in this part of the ballpark and as I walked farther, I heard the beautiful music of Mark Knopfler and Dire Straits.

"Outside a door, I heard what I thought was ping pong balls and before I could turn around and walk away, not wanting to be seen, Vinny opened the door.

"Vinny asked if he could help me and as I fumbled for words, I saw Rusty and he saw me."

Rusty was now sitting in between Meghan and Sally at this point and Louise looked over at him. Rusty nodded as if to say he knows what story she's about to end with. Louise grinned back and continued.

"Why Vinny opened the door that day at that moment, I have no idea. He was and still is the keeper of the flame, the ultimate connector, the one who wants everyone else to have fun, to bring their best self to the party. Once he saw I was there, he welcomed me into Rusty's grounds crew clubhouse.

"I knew of Rusty and we had seen each other around the ballpark. I can't say we ever had a conversation until that day, yet there I was. Vinny was thrilled to have a visitor and Rusty was a gracious leader who welcomed me into their office headquarters.

"That day happened to be their grounds crew ping pong championship. Other than Vinny and Rusty, the room remained focused on the heated game. Big John was in the corner with a thick book, reading away.

"Rusty gave me a quick tour, and near the end, I saw the white athletic tape above the exit: **Push the Tarp**. I asked and before Rusty could answer, Vinny gave me a rundown of the three pillars of the framework: how we all show up, how we all push and how we keep pushing.

"I had never heard of a culture or mindset framed in this way. I was captivated by the mantra and the symbol of the tarp. I was about to be on my way when

Rusty said, 'If you don't mind, Louise, what brought you down this way today?'

"I explained that my walk was driven by my panic about having to speak in public. Rusty replied with 'How do you get to Carnegie Hall?' and Vinny jumped in with perfect timing: 'Practice, practice, practice!'

"Rusty and Vinny talked me through the pillar of persistence and it being about staying present, being enthusiastic and passionate, and putting in the practice.

"I'm sure you agree that being in the moment is much easier when you're comfortable. It's when we are uneasy about a new task, a skill not yet developed, a conversation we've never had...that's when it's hard to stay present, and you can quickly forget about your passion.

"The difference maker for me since that very day has been practicing with purpose. Rusty helped me learn that if you bring yourself to practice and put in the time purposefully, you can deepen your skills, acquire new abilities and accomplish great things in your life's journey.

"Rusty suggested I start by talking in front of a mirror and Vinny recommended writing and rewriting my remarks in bullet format. With these suggestions, I thanked both of them and started to walk out. I took one step and heard someone say, 'Turn up the music loud, too!'

"Rusty asked Big John for clarity and John said to practice with loud music to heighten my focus and sharpen my remarks. 'Bad music, too!'

"I came to learn Big John's uncle was a pastor in Davenport and always rehearsed his Sunday sermons with a record playing very loud.

"That's my final suggestion: practice, practice, practice. You may not end up in Carnegie Hall but you'll challenge yourself to be the best you can be. As your skills improve, keep surrounding yourself with friends, colleagues and mentors who will keep challenging you to reach even greater levels of mastery."

Louise was fantastic that night. I remember Rusty sitting with Meghan and Sally, all three with a look of pure contentment. I could tell he was getting emotional because he was doing that thing where he started looking away.

As Louise thanked everyone and wished everyone the best of luck, Harry offered that if anyone had a quick question or two for Louise to ask before she left to grab a late dinner with Rusty.

As the Chinooks clapped, a few hustled over to Louise and the others started to clean up the dugout and put everything away in the storage closet.

Rusty and I walked with Meghan and Sally to wait for their parents to pick up the girls after their ice cream run. I thanked Rusty for that night and for the previous several weeks. He said, "Jimmy, it's been a pleasure. To be honest, you've helped me as much as I've helped you. You and Harry have given me a renewed purpose after Susan passed. Thank God for my son, Patrick, and daughter-in-law, Kate, but they didn't know what to do with me, either.

"Now it's up to you to bring Push the Tarp forward in your way. Remember: your journey is your race."

The Bowmans' car was pulling up at the exact time Louise came over. Meghan and Sally thanked Louise and hugged me for a great night. I told the Bowmans I'd be right behind them.

Before I walked to my car, I thanked Louise for being so generous with her time and for sharing her story. I remarked that Vinny and Big John sounded like real characters with character.

Louise and Rusty both laughed, and Rusty said, "They couldn't be more different, and I was so blessed to work with them. They are both the very best. They know about you, Jimmy. They both want to meet you someday."

With that I said good night and started walking to my car. Louise popped her SUV hatch so Rusty could throw his bike in the back and off they went.

CHAPTER 27
BLACK COFFEE

In the past when I would have exciting nights like the night I just had with the Chinooks, Rusty and Louise, I would have been wired and unable to sleep. That night, however, I fell asleep as my head hit the pillow. Maybe it was the four weeks of being up at sunrise, or maybe it was the bittersweet feeling that I would be meeting with Rusty for our final session.

I never could have imagined the opportunities that my broken wrist would have provided to me. I was able to learn one on one from a legend in a part of the country I had never visited.

I also became a part of the Bowman family and saw the game of baseball from a different vantage point.

That next morning I hopped out of bed at 4:45, committed to getting to the dugout before Rusty, once and for all. I brought with me two cups of black coffee—one for Rusty and one for me as a sign of my formal entrance to the 5 a.m. Club.

To my delight, I arrived at the Chinooks ballpark and did not see Rusty's bike leaning up against the back of the third-base dugout. It was raining so I thought the old sage may have brought his bike into the dugout.

I realized I had done it. For our very last session, I was the early bird and with coffee for both of us. I sat on the bench and sipped my coffee slowly, waiting for

Rusty as the early morning rain created a soothing playlist for my morning victory.

It was 5:15 and I expected to hear the now familiar sound of Rusty cycling to the Chinooks park a short few miles from Patrick and Kate's home.

And then I waited. At 5:30 I remember thinking that maybe his dinner with Louise the previous night ran late and he was moving slower this morning.

Then I waited and waited and waited.

No Rusty.

It was almost 6 a.m. and I had a bad feeling in my gut.

Maybe someone hit him on the way to our session. I was running all kinds of thoughts through my head when Harry turned the corner. Instead of his usual enthusiasm, he looked like he had seen a ghost.

He saw me and said, "Jimmy—hey pal." He paused and struggled for the words as he walked toward me. "Rusty died in his sleep last night. I was on my way to work out and his son, Patrick, called me. I rushed over there and when I arrived the coroner was already there."

I was stunned. I felt like I was underwater and that this was a bad dream. I ran my hand through my hair and felt Harry put one hand on my right shoulder. He thumped down next to me as we both stared out at the rain. We sat in relative silence for the next half hour or so. We cried and we wondered why.

Rusty's cup of coffee sat next to us.

After a while, Harry stood up. He needed to schedule a team meeting and said he would include me on the text so I knew where and when it would happen...likely right where I was sitting.

"Oh, Jimmy," Harry said, "I almost forgot. Patrick gave this to me to give to you. It was on Rusty's night table this morning."

Harry handed me Rusty's index card that he got from Charlie on his first day of work—the one he kept in his wallet all those years that had layers of scotch tape to preserve the folded treasure. On the back of the card in black marker, Rusty wrote,

> *Dear Jimmy - welcome to the 5 a.m. Club.*
> *Your future is bright. Keep pushing the*
> *tarp. Your friend, Rusty.*

Tears rolled down my cheeks as I held the card and thought of our time together. Among all of the sadness and grief were bittersweet feelings of immense gratitude for all the gifts he gave me.

In one month he helped me in countless ways. Rusty was a storyteller and a leader. Over his years he developed an ability to synthesize what matters and to let go of what doesn't.

Not only did he encompass the elements of service, teamwork and persistence, but also the blending of those qualities in his authentic way.

For Rusty, magic happened when those three pillars fused together. They made each other stronger, brighter and more beautiful.

I sat for a while longer before I called my dad. He and my mom said they would fly out for the services once we knew the details.

I dreaded going back to the Bowmans to share the news with them. I made my way to my car, leaving Rusty's black coffee behind.

The days that followed were a blur. My parents arrived and stayed at a nearby hotel. The Chinooks took two days off and mourned the loss of our mentor.

Harry showed a different side of his leadership as he made sure we all spent even more time together.

Thursday was the funeral. It started with a one-hour viewing and then a mass. All of this took place in Milwaukee at Church of the Gesu on the campus of Marquette University.

Rusty did not go to college but I learned that almost his entire family were Marquette alumni and Rusty was a close friend of the Jesuits, the Catholic order that founded Marquette in 1881 and remains today.

I picked up my parents at their hotel and we walked into the church with the Bowmans. Meghan and Sally were sad but resolute to say farewell to "Mr. Rusty," as Sally put it.

Rusty's entire family was in town and I was struck by their humility and togetherness. Rusty's son, Patrick, and I saw one another and he gave me a big hug when we got to the front of the family's receiving line.

He wanted to be sure Harry delivered his dad's note to me and I assured him he did. I thanked Patrick for sharing his dad with me and he said it was the best thing for him. Patrick said, "The Chinooks were like medicine for Dad. He was lost without mom and the Chinooks were a gift. And Harry is hard to turn down, too! Jimmy, he thought the world of you. He said you were very eager to learn and he came home last night on top of the world."

Moments after we were seated, the Chinooks walked in as a team, led by Harry. All of them. Together. Minutes later came a who's who in Milwaukee baseball history. One baseball great after another humbly paid their respects to the man who helped set their stage for decades of Milwaukee baseball.

Louise arrived along with Jay Johnston and all of the front office executive team, past and present. Louise and Jay sat up front in the pew behind the family.

I guessed who Vinny was from Rusty's stories. Vinny gave anyone near him a huge hug and was noticeably managing swings of nostalgia mixed with deep anguish from the sudden death of his mentor and close friend.

Big John was the very last person down the line before mass started. Maybe he wanted it that way. He started on Charlie's crew the same day as Rusty and now he was preparing to say goodbye. He was farm-boy strong, indeed. He was older than the picture I had of him in my head. He wore a sharp navy suit, white shirt and royal blue tie. He marched methodically down the aisle ever so slowly, looking at the pictures assembled on easels by Rusty's family. Big John made it through the family receiving line and when he sat down, the family took their seats and the mass began.

Patrick said his dad would have been so grateful for this turnout at Gesu, and he would be saying that we all should have something better to do. It was a nod to Rusty's dry humor and big smile—the smile that wore those creases on his face.

Louise approached the lectern next and spoke lovingly of her dear friend. What a public speaker she had become over the years. She eulogized the friend she came to know that fateful afternoon when she was terrified about her first public speaking event. Louise shared a little of that day and elicited a laugh with Rusty's Carnegie Hall joke.

She spoke of his gift as a leader for seeing the best in people and realizing their talents before they saw it in themselves. How he could create a framework, first derived from the great Charlie Keyes, that we now know as *Push the Tarp*, and have the trust and grounded confidence for his teams to develop it in new and evolving ways through the years. It wasn't his system alone. He shared it with all of us.

She reminded everyone that while we are all devastated to lose him, he is happily reunited with his Susan—the love of his life.

Big John, Vinny and Harry served as pallbearers along with members of his family as mourners followed the casket carrying Rusty to his final resting place at a private burial.

Before the mass concluded, Patrick invited everyone to the Milwaukee Athletic Club for a celebration of life luncheon.

CHAPTER 29
THANK YOU AND FAREWELL

The Bowmans headed home but my parents and I made our way from Marquette to the Milwaukee Athletic Club for Rusty's farewell luncheon.

The room was crowded with friends, family and colleagues who wanted to gather and pay tribute to a life well lived. Patrick welcomed us and invited guests to take to the microphone and tell a story about Rusty, toast his life, and describe the impact he had on everyone.

The stories went on for quite some time and ended with Vinny telling about Rusty teaching himself Spanish online and learning how to play guitar...how Rusty never stopped learning and growing, and how curious he was to know his colleagues on a deep level.

Vinny said having Rusty in his life was a true gift. He made special mention of Charlie Keyes and Big John and how his generation and the ones coming up have not only a debt of gratitude but an important responsibility to carry forward the tenets of Push the Tarp. Big John didn't move other than to raise his glass toward Vinny as he sat at a back table looking respectfully at him.

Vinny said, "Rusty lives with us in the culture he has taught us to foster, for those we lead and those we get to work with in our life. He empowered us to be ourselves and he never missed a chance to let us know he cared."

Vinny was himself an engaging speaker and he paused at that point and looked at the ground as he choked back tears.

Vinny ended with a nod to Harry (who was in the room) and the Chinooks for the joy we all brought Rusty these last weeks of his life. Vinny said he called Rusty often and Rusty told him all about the team, Coach Harry and a special project he was working on.

"To family, friends and to Rusty. Cheers." So ended the speaking portion of the luncheon.

Vinny and a few former teammates made a playlist to best honor Rusty, with a healthy dose of all types of music. I noticed plenty of Dire Straits and the first time Mark Knopfler's voice was heard, I saw Vinny walk over to Louise and give her a hug.

Pictures of Rusty with Susan, with his family, and with his teammates surrounded the room. The meal featured some of Rusty's favorite foods, too. Patrick had it catered from a cookbook Rusty's team gifted him last year at his retirement party.

Former colleagues came from all over the country to pay their respects. Vinny and Big John and Louise were joined by over a hundred teammates who once worked with or for Rusty.

Big John drove up from Davenport by himself. The mutual respect between John and Rusty was limitless.

They were brothers. I wanted to walk over and introduce myself and couldn't muster the courage.

That's when I saw Louise talking with Vinny and I thought that would be a good time to introduce myself before it was time to drive my folks to the airport.

I politely joined their standing conversation in the middle of the room and shared my condolences to Louise and said what a moving eulogy she gave for Rusty.

Vinny jumped right in with, "Well you must be Rusty's special project! Jimmy, it's great to meet you. I've heard so much about you from Rusty."

I thanked Vinny and told him everything Rusty shared about him. I also said I was a big fan of the Lou Piniella story.

"He told you the Lou Piniella story? That's great. Cap got a kick out of that story. It's true, too. My dad, God rest his soul, and Cap hit it off. Whenever my parents came to town, Cap and Susan took them to dinner."

I saw Louise's eyes widen as she looked over Vinny's shoulder. Big John was on the move and he put his giant hand on Vinny's shoulder. "Nice job, Vin," he said. "You, too, Louise. Your eulogy was right on. You've come a long way." Then he gave her a Big John hug.

"Thank you, John," Louise replied gratefully. "I was wondering when I was up there if you were going to start playing the organ to test my game."

Big John laughed and turned to me. "You must be Jimmy. Your cast gives it away." I replied "Yes, very nice to meet you, John." Before I could say anything else, Big John continued: "Jimmy, you're due for a visit to Davenport. I'll have to fill in all the holes with the stories Rusty left out." Then he winked at Vinny and Louise and walked toward Patrick to say goodbye. He did turn back briefly to ask me, "Jimmy, do you play chess?" I responded, "Yes, sir" and he simply said, "Good," as he approached Rusty's family.

Big John said one last goodbye to Patrick and Rusty's extended family. Next he walked over to the manager at the club and asked him to play a song. He made his way to the ballroom exit and turned around to wait for the music to start.

The song is hard for me to listen to these days without thinking of Rusty and tearing up.

The lyrics and melody of *Gentle on My Mind,* by Billy Bragg and Joe Henry, tugs at my heart strings. Louise and Vinny were talking with each other while I had a straight line of sight to Big John standing in the doorway. He took up most of it. I can only imagine all the hours he and Rusty spent together through the years. Pushing the tarp in the rain and in the heat and together with Charlie, they built a system that would someday outlive all of them and impact countless people.

The song was a sweet way for Rusty's celebration of life to wind down. I noticed Big John welling up in tears as he looked up at the ceiling and slowly clapped his right hand flatly on his left a few times. He walked out the door just as the song ended, to begin his drive back to Davenport. It was his way of saying thank you and farewell to Rusty.

It meant a lot to me that my parents came to the service for Rusty. Ironically and sadly, they met everyone but him. They also have a new appreciation for the beauty of Wisconsin.

I dropped them off and drove straight from the airport to the Chinooks ballpark. The flags were already at half-staff and Harry was walking alone on the field.

Harry was a great coach. I grew to appreciate that he wasn't a rah-rah yeller and screamer. If you spent time with Harry, his kindness is what shined most. He loved the game and was eager to share the game with his players. His genuine enthusiasm was contagious. He made you feel appreciated. He made you better.

I approached him in front of the third-base dugout. "Harry," I said, careful not to startle him, as he seemed to be with his thoughts in another place. "Jimmy," he replied softly. "How are you doing, pal?"

"I'm not that great, I guess. I still can't believe he's gone. He was really special. He made me think of things in a different way and he's inspired me to take what I learned this last month and put it to work for my last year of college and beyond."

I also wanted to share my appreciation for Harry. "Harry, I wouldn't have been here this last month if it weren't for you. You convinced Rusty to help the team and without your kindness, I wouldn't have met you, the team, the Bowmans or Rusty."

Harry responded, "Jimmy...like Rusty knew, 'it's all in front of you.' Bring the elements of Push the Tarp with you and live out your dreams. As you do it, you will impact more people than you ever imagined. Trust me, the world needs leaders like you. Pay it forward. Help the Meghans and the Sallys coming up behind us and inspire them to do the same in their own ways. It's been a pleasure to meet you, to learn from you and have you with us this last month. Stay in touch and know I'm always here if I can help you in any way."

That night, the Chinooks honored their mentor. Patrick and his family rode their bikes from their home to the diamond in honor of Rusty, whose bike was omnipresent at the ballpark. Not many noticed until the national anthem started that Harry had leaned Rusty's bike against the flagpole. The bike stayed there for the rest of the season.

Johnson demanded to start on only four days' rest. He pitched three innings of no hit ball and after walking the first runner in the fourth inning, Harry made a pitching change. The Chinooks won easily, 8-1. I said my goodbyes to the team that night and had ice cream one last time with the Bowmans.

The flight home was uneventful. I remembered journaling some on the flight back to LaGuardia and I couldn't get *Gentle on My Mind* out of my head.

SENIOR SEASON

CHAPTER 31
SENIOR SEASON

My senior year of college was different from my previous three. It flew by quickly. Harry and the Bowmans surprised me and came to my last home game of my college career. Harry even set it up with Coach Delancey so the girls could be bat girls.

Upon graduation I had a trip scheduled to Davenport, Iowa. Big John was waiting to onboard me in his version of this system and I couldn't have been more excited. After two weeks in Davenport, I was off to San Francisco to start my post-college career as a new member of Vinny's grounds crew.

I had moments of bittersweet thoughts, like when I awoke at 5:15 a.m. each day and wanted to call Rusty. Or when I visited the Bowmans and checked out a Chinooks game to see Harry and somehow hoped Rusty would be there.

I knew he wouldn't be. What I also knew, because of my time with Rusty that summer, is that *the journey is the destination*.

I knew that Push the Tarp is a mindset for leaders and teams to create an environment where people feel like they matter and that they are part of something greater than themselves...that they can be great teammates and also not have all of the answers or possess every skill...that great teammates lean on each other and blindly trust that they can.

123

And that if we keep pushing and stay in the pocket of our pursuits, we will grow and learn with teammates and colleagues, family and friends, mentors and mentees and pursue the best version of ourselves while we positively impact more people than we ever imagined we could.

Vinny - Vinny became an anchor in the Bay Area, known not only for his great leadership of the San Francisco grounds crew but also as the founder of the *Institute for Grounded Confidence*.

He is known lovingly as *Vulnerable Vinny* and speaks widely on the importance of vulnerable leaders and teams. He believes that vulnerability is the beginning.

He lives in the Bay Area with his wife, Sandy, and three kids: Brian, Sean and Barrett, and their yellow Lab, Lou.

Big John - After many years with Charlie and Rusty in Milwaukee, John served as grounds crew chief for the top minor league organization in Des Moines, Iowa. Three years ago, he retired to his hometown of Davenport, Iowa, where he is an assistant librarian and high school chess coach.

He started a book club with former colleagues from his days in Milwaukee. He also sings in his church choir every Sunday, where his uncle once served as pastor.

Louise - She continued to lead the front office in Milwaukee and served 15 years as GM. When she retired, six professional baseball organizations had women in general manager roles.

Louise stayed active in retirement, writing books and speaking internationally at conferences, corporate retreats and leadership summits. She often framed her talks around relationships, trust and purposeful practice...and she always mentioned Rusty and the mindset of Push the Tarp.

Meghan - After aging out of being a bat girl, Meghan went on to star at Florida State in softball as a first team All-American selection and member of the Dean's List as a dual major in psychology and English.

After graduation, she earned a master's in counseling at UT-Austin and enjoyed a fellowship as a lead instructor at Vinny's *Institute for Grounded Confidence*.

Sally - Earned an engineering degree at Marquette University and later a master's and PhD at Northwestern University in biomedical engineering. She continued her academic career at Marquette and later became the first woman to serve as dean of the college of engineering. She also purchased the Chinooks and runs it to this day as one of the top summer collegiate baseball organizations in the United States.

Johnson - Johnson went on to pitch 12 years in the big leagues for three organizations. He credits much of his success to the summer with Rusty and Harry. You would find *Push The Tarp* stitched on his glove for his entire professional career.

Harry - A lifelong resident of Mequon, Wisconsin, he remains the summer coach for the Chinooks. Vinny, Big John and Louise visit regularly. Every game day, one of the Chinooks players is selected to lean Rusty's bike against the flagpole as a remembrance of his legacy and impact.

Jimmy - To be continued...

THE PUSH THE TARP FRAMEWORK

Three pillars of framework:

1. We *Show Up* (Service)
2. We *Push the Tarp* (Teamwork)
3. We *Keep Pushing* (Persistence)

WE *SHOW* UP (SERVICE)

- **Love and care**
- **Humility**
- **Mission-driven**

WE *PUSH THE TARP* (TEAMWORK)

- **Connected**
- **Vulnerable**
- **Execute our roles**

WE *KEEP PUSHING* (PERSISTENCE)

- **Present**
- **Passionate**
- **Practice**

QUESTIONS FOR REFLECTION

(#1) <u>CHAPTER 9:</u> What are the three elements of *service*? Which of the three resonates most with you? Why?

(#2) <u>CHAPTER 11:</u> Why did Push the Tarp written in black marker on white athletic tape matter to Rusty and his teams? What does it showcase?

(#3) <u>CHAPTER 13:</u> What strategies and tactics did Jimmy witness Harry employ to serve his Chinook players?

(#4) CHAPTER 14: How did Vinny connect with his teammates? What was it that made him a vulnerable teammate?

(#5) CHAPTER 15: Why do you think Rusty liked the Lou Piniella story so much?

(#6) CHAPTER 16: Why did it matter to Big John and Rusty that *everyone* pushes the tarp?

(#7) CHAPTER 18: What did the quiet hour allow Jimmy to do? What is valuable about having a quiet morning routine?

(#8) CHAPTER 19: What are the three P's of *persistence*? What are some of the strategies mentioned in Push the Tarp that you will try?

(#9) CHAPTER 23: What was Good! about the Chinooks' win against the Racine Generals?

(#10) CHAPTER 24: What did Louise mean when she said to "Run your race"?

(#11) CHAPTER 25: What persistence strategy did Rusty, Vinny and Big John help Louise with? Why does Big John tell Louise to turn the music up loud?

(#12) CHAPTER 27: What's the significance of the black coffee Jimmy brings to the dugout? What pillar of Push the Tarp is he providing to Rusty?

(#13) CHAPTER 29: Why did Big John play that particular song at the memorial luncheon? What do you think he was trying to communicate?

(#14) Throughout the book: What are some of the relationships you enjoy the most between the characters? Why?

138

ABOUT THE AUTHOR

Tim McMahon serves as vice president for university advancement at Marquette University in Milwaukee, Wisconsin.

He leads an outstanding team of advancement professionals focused on Pushing the Tarp with a culture of Service, Teamwork and Persistence.

Tim brings more than 20 years of experience from prior roles at Villanova, Hofstra and Fordham universities.

He earned a BBA in marketing from Hofstra's Zarb School of Business (where he was a member of the baseball program) and an MBA from Fordham University's Gabelli School of Business.

He lives in Mequon with his wife, Kara, their three boys and a yellow Lab. Beyond work, Tim is an avid reader and writer who loves to travel and play golf, chess and pickleball.

CONNECT WITH TIM & PUSH THE TARP

@TF_McMahon
@PushTheTarp

/PushTheTarp

/Tim-McMahon

/PushTheTarp

@tfmcmahon218
@PushTheTarp

CONTACT TIM

Contact Tim to inquire about having him come speak with your team, school or organization so you can Push *Your* Tarp. Tim delivers his message with energy and enthusiasm to help educate, empower and inspire his audiences. If you are looking for a keynote speaker who will energize your team/staff and leave them with simple and powerful strategies to optimize their mindset, leadership and culture while accelerating results, contact Tim today.

Contact Tim by visiting
PushTheTarp.com or on Social Media

PUSH THE TARP PLAYLIST
Available In Spotify By Searching
Push The Tarp Playlist

1. "Start Me Up" - The Rolling Stones
2. "Fool in the Rain" - Led Zeppelin
3. "It's a Great Day to be Alive" – Travis Tritt
4. "Same Boat" – Zac Brown Band
5. "Walk of Life" - Dire Straits
6. "Burning Down the House" - Talking Heads
7. "Washing Dishes" - Jack Johnson
8. "Walking in Memphis" - Marc Cohn
9. "This Is Us" - Mark Knopfler and Emmylou Harris
10. "Stand by Me" - Billy Bragg and Joe Henry
11. "Gentle on My Mind" – Billy Bragg, Joe Henry
12. "Feelin' Alright" – Joe Cocker

Made in the USA
Middletown, DE
05 July 2022